QUESTIONING TECHNIQUE
Pocketbook

By Gorden Pope

Cartoons:
Phil Hailstone

Published by:

Teachers' Pocketbooks
Laurel House, Station Approach,
Alresford, Hampshire SO24 9JH, UK
Tel: +44 (0)1962 735573
Fax: +44 (0)1962 733637
Email: sales@teacherspocketbooks.co.uk
Website: www.teacherspocketbooks.co.uk

Teachers' Pocketbooks is an imprint of
Management Pocketbooks Ltd.

Series editor – Linda Edge

© Gorden Pope 2013

This edition published 2013. Reprinted 2014.
ISBN 978 1 906610 50 0

E-book ISBN 978 1 908284 98 3

British Library Cataloguing-in-Publication Data
– A catalogue record for this book is available
from the British Library.

Design, typesetting and graphics by Efex Ltd.
Printed in UK.

Contents

Foreword

'The whole sum of what may be said about questioning is comprised in this: It ought to set the learners thinking, to promote activity and energy on their parts, and to arouse the whole mental faculty into action instead of blindly cultivating the memory at the expense of the higher intellectual powers.'

The Art of Teaching
Sir Joshua G Fitch
1824 – 1903

Foreword

Questioning is a teacher's bread and butter. It is an area of teaching characterised by a great deal of instinctive practice, which many think of as an innate skill. We do it hundreds of times a day, day in day out. Teachers I meet are highly aware of the effect that good questioning has on student thinking and learning. They understand the fallacy of *cultivating the memory at the expense of the higher cognitive powers*, particularly in these times of information overload. They know that one of the most useful attributes we can develop in young people is the ability to think critically and maintain a healthy scepticism. Teachers' questions play a critical role, not just for the thinking they provoke, but in the modelling of questioning skills and strategies and the development of curiosity.

And yet, despite acknowledging the importance of questioning, teachers all too often rely on intuition and thinking on their feet. Whilst these are desirable traits in the hurly-burly of the classroom, questioning can be so much more effective.

Foreword

Teachers often say that they don't have time to plan questions, don't see it as a necessity and take pride in their ability to ask good questions 'off the cuff'. Yet the research shows time and again that when we think more about our questioning, when we deepen our understanding, extend our range of strategies and then plan with questioning in mind, the responses from pupils improve, and engagement and learning increase.

This is a book for all involved in the teaching profession – whether you are new to teaching or have been 'at it' for some time, this Pocketbook will provide you with models, strategies, tips and techniques along with much food for thought about developing your own practice. It is based on up-to-date research and thinking, looking at what works best. It adds to ideas you have met before and offers new ways to look at this ancient teaching technique. In separating out the elements of questioning – framing questions, delivering them and responding to the answers – it provides a host of ideas to try, from simple tweaks to fundamental shifts.

Raising
Questions

 The Questioning
Environment

 Framing
Questions

 Delivering
the Question

 Responding to
the Answer

 Improving
Your Practice

Raising
Questions

The importance of questions

Questioning is an absolutely interactive process that performs so many functions it's no surprise that it's the most researched aspect of teaching and learning. Imagine trying to teach without asking questions. You would be unable to develop pupils' understanding and, even if you suspected you had, you wouldn't be able to check what or how much they knew.

In this section you can see the various purposes teachers have for asking questions. With these in mind you can check which you use most and least often, with a view to extending your repertoire.

We'll also look at a variety of frameworks for classifying questions. It is often reported that teachers ask questions that lead their pupils only to lower level memory and recall. By familiarising ourselves with different ways of categorising the cognitive levels that questions are pitched at we can plan questions on the basis of the mental activity or intellectual behaviour we want to develop.

Why ask questions?

The reasons for asking questions are plentiful. We use them to:

- Summarise and review previously learned material
- Draw individuals into the lesson
- Demonstrate that pupils are expected to be active participants
- Focus pupils on key issues or concepts
- Arouse curiosity
- Determine how much the class understands – to pitch lessons at appropriate level
- Diagnose specific difficulties
- Help pupils to reflect on information and commit it to memory
- Learn vicariously while listening to discussion
- Develop pupils' reflection and comment on others' responses
- Develop thinking skills
- Encourage discussion
- Stimulate new ideas
- Develop from concrete and factual to analytical and evaluative
- Help pupils see connections and relationships
- Model how experienced learners seek meaning

Expert teachers are clear about the purpose of the question they are asking.

How do questions stimulate learning?

Teachers have long known that pupils are not empty vessels to be filled with facts. The theory of learning known as **constructivism** tells us that learning happens through experience and reflection – making a construct.

When we encounter new information we compare it with what we know already, our previous ideas and experiences. We then change or modify what we believed, or dismiss it. We create our own knowledge. Where the new experience conflicts with the existing, we experience **cognitive conflict** and either assimilate the new information into our existing constructs or accommodate it, creating a new construct.

More on cognitive conflict

Example

Children will readily tell you that wrapping a hot item in wool will help it to stay warmer longer, but they resist the notion that wrapping something cold in wool will help it stay cold longer. The struggle with apparent incongruity is one way we make sense of the world.

Questioning and dialogue are highly effective ways of generating cognitive conflict to build new learning, and of identifying the misunderstandings that constructing our own meaning can cause.

Therefore, effective teachers use questioning to both **extend** and to **monitor** thinking.

The Zone of Proximal Development

Linked to constructivism and cognitive conflict is Vygotsky's **Zone of Proximal Development** (ZPD). The ZPD is the difference between what a child can do independently and what they can do with help. The child follows the adult (or more capable peer) and gradually develops the ability to do the task independently.

By giving you clues about misunderstandings and misconstructions, questions play an important part in identifying a pupil's ZPD and, consequently, what they need to do / learn next. They also provide an opportunity for modelling thinking skills.

Later in the book we'll be looking at strategies that support constructivist teaching, eg 'think, pair, share', examining wrong answers, group discussion, Socratic questioning higher order thinking questions, all-pupil engagement strategies.

What is effective questioning?

When questioning is at its most effective it:

- Reinforces and revisits learning objectives
- Maintains the flow of learning in the lesson
- Includes staged sequences of questions
- Involves all pupils
- Engages pupils in thinking for themselves
- Encourages pupils to speculate and hypothesise
- Promotes justification and reasoning
- Encourages creative thought and imaginative and innovative thinking

- Models higher order thinking
- Creates an atmosphere of trust where pupils' opinions and ideas are valued
- Shows connections between previous and new learning
- Encourages pupils to listen and respond to each other as well as the teacher
- Seeks the views and opinions of students
- Engages the emotions
- Creates a sense of shared learning

Frameworks and classifications

On the following pages are a number of taxonomies, frameworks and classifications of levels of thinking and types of question. Categorising thinking and questioning helps us to understand what types of thinking we are requiring of students when we ask certain types of question. We can then make sure we ask enough higher order questions and that we choose the right question for the purpose.

The point about frameworks like these is that they help you to be specific about the level of cognitive processing you require, ie how challenging your question is. Unless you have made a firm decision that a question is aiming at a particular level, it is very easy for a potentially higher order question to be diluted by a factually correct answer. If you have determined in advance the level of response you are looking for, you can follow up with a probing question to extend the pupil's thinking and answer.

Theories and models

1. The original Bloom's Taxonomy of Educational Objectives

No book about questioning would be complete without a reference to Benjamin Bloom's *Taxonomy of Educational Objectives*. Created in 1957, it has stood the test of time and is still regarded as a key classification model.

Bloom's taxonomy describes **analysis**, **synthesis** and **evaluation** as the 'higher order thinking skills' so often referred to and which make such a difference when used in questioning. There is debate about the hierarchical order of those three, some arguing that they are equal. The revised version (see page 18) swaps synthesis and evaluation. But, in practical terms, since all three are 'higher order' it is an academic argument.

1. The original Bloom

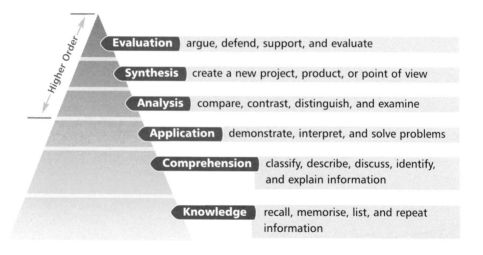

Higher Order

Evaluation argue, defend, support, and evaluate

Synthesis create a new project, product, or point of view

Analysis compare, contrast, distinguish, and examine

Application demonstrate, interpret, and solve problems

Comprehension classify, describe, discuss, identify, and explain information

Knowledge recall, memorise, list, and repeat information

1. The original Bloom

Bloom's taxonomy has become a stalwart in the stock of teachers' resources. It provides a logical way of categorising (in our case, questions) to identify the type of thinking required.

Knowing which type of thinking your questions will provoke means you can keep a balance between higher and lower order thinking and between the different higher order categories. Planning your questioning will ensure that you do not default to your personal preferences.

In 2001 Anderson and Krathwohl revised Bloom's taxonomy. They made a number of additions and a significant change that make the revised taxonomy more useful...

2. The revised Bloom

… Anderson and Krathwohl argued that 'knowledge' is not a cognitive level at all; rather it is present within each level as it drives the thinking. Their revision removes knowledge from the cognitive domain altogether:

The Cognitive Process Dimension

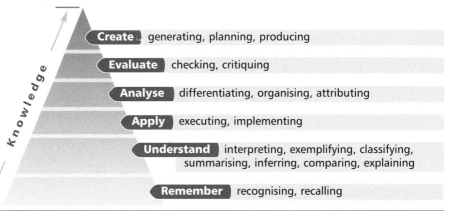

Knowledge

Create generating, planning, producing

Evaluate checking, critiquing

Analyse differentiating, organising, attributing

Apply executing, implementing

Understand interpreting, exemplifying, classifying, summarising, inferring, comparing, explaining

Remember recognising, recalling

2. The revised Bloom

The knowledge dimension now pervades all six levels and comes in four domains.

The Knowledge Dimension

Factual knowledge

terminology, specific details, elements

Conceptual knowledge

concepts, categories, classifications, theories

Procedural knowledge

skills, algorithms, techniques, methods

Meta-cognitive knowledge

personal learning and thinking, self-assessment, self-monitoring

So you will be using a particular knowledge domain at a particular cognitive level. You can of course be using more than one knowledge domain at a time and working at more than one cognitive level at a time.

3. Gallagher and Ascher's questioning taxonomy

Gallagher and Ascher's questioning taxonomy from 1963 describes four question levels in ascending order of challenge.

1. Cognitive memory questions
recognition, rote memory, selective recall.

▶ *What were the names of Henry VIII's wives?*

2. Convergent thinking questions
analysing, integrating data, closed questions, but with analysis.

▶ *Which is more economical, car or train from Dover to Glasgow?*

3. Divergent thinking questions
independently generated data or a new perspective on a given topic. More than one possible answer.

▶ *What addition and multiplication problems could lead to the answer 16?*

4. Evaluative thinking questions
matters of judgment, value, and choice.

▶ *Which is the best school in the area?*

4. The Sternberg model

Robert Sternberg designed his Triarchic theory in 1997 and developed it further in 2008. Unlike the other models we've looked at where the thinking increases in complexity as you move up the taxonomy, Sternberg's is not hierarchical – here you cannot say that one type of thinking is more or less complex than the others.

Analytic – analysing, evaluating, criticising, reasoning, and judging. *To what extent is digging holes as punishment like detention?*	Learner is required to compare and contrast.
Creative – discovering, inventing, dealing with novelty, and creating. *How could the author have made the ending more positive?*	Learner is required to use imagination.
Practical – implying, implementing, and using. *Why do you think Stanley gives X-Ray the lipstick tube? What would you have done if you were in Stanley's place?*	Learner is required to empathise.
Wisdom – moral judgement, values. *Stanley's father, an inventor, says, 'I learn from failure'. What could this mean? In what ways have you learned from failure?*	Learner is required to use life experience and wisdom to apply a general principle to a specific example.

From theory to practice – beyond Bloom

> *Inspectors must consider whether... ... teachers use questioning and discussion to assess the effectiveness of their teaching and promote pupils' learning.*
> **2012 School Inspection Handbook (Ofsted)**

There is a multitude of ways to categorise questions and their functions. Whichever way you look at it, an awareness and understanding of these will help you to develop your questioning skills. Practise your techniques, allow time for discussion and be explicit about the learning that is taking place.

The important thing is to match the type of question to the level of cognitive challenge you are seeking to promote. Keep it in mind and if the answer you receive doesn't reach your target, probe, push and question further, using whole class, small group and individual questions to maximise learning.

Look back over the frameworks outlined in the previous pages. Which do you prefer? How about trying something new?

Raising
Questions

 The Questioning
Environment ◄

 Framing
Questions

 Delivering
the Question

 Responding to
the Answer

 Improving
Your Practice

The Questioning
Environment

The right climate

There's more to effective questioning than asking good questions at the right time. If your students are fearful of making mistakes, uncertain of what is required, or simply not interested, then your virtuoso questions will fall on stony ground. Hand in hand with your skills as a questioner is the learning culture you create.

So before we get into the detail of specific questioning strategies, this chapter looks at the learning environment and how your questioning can determine its character. What factors contribute to an effective questioning environment?

- Learning is a supportive, not competitive, process of understanding
- Students listen to and support each other
- Teacher and pupils explore wrong answers
- Everyone is comfortable with 'Wait Time'
- Pupils supportively challenge each other
- Students are confident to take risks and share partly-formed thinking
- Students' opinions and values are sought as well as facts and solutions
- Discussion moves from one student to another, not always through the teacher
- Everyone is engaged

Setting the rules

You probably spend some time at the beginning of each year negotiating the class rules, a class contract or 'golden rules'. Somewhere in these rules will be one or two that relate to how students respond to your questions. When agreeing the rules you might illustrate them with examples based on a questioning situation, so that your students see how potentially abstract ideas work in practice:

- *'Treat others as you want to be treated yourself'* translates to *'Listen with respect'*
- *'Try your best'* translates to *'When asked a question, 'don't know' is not good enough'*
- Sharing statements include *'sharing the floor in a discussion'*
- Teasing and bullying include *'ridiculing wrong answers'*

Make a point of talking about the fact that all contributions are respected, that sometimes the most unlikely sounding idea turns out to be the most productive and that everyone is expected to think about the questions you ask.

Which of your classroom rules can relate to answering questions?

Fear of mistakes

Many students, across the ability range, fear making mistakes and are reluctant to take risks. This includes giving a wrong answer in front of the class, or expressing an idea that is not accepted or valued by their friends. It is not the fear of being wrong in itself; it is of looking silly, being ridiculed. **'Peer fear'** is a significant barrier in many classrooms.

Counter-intuitively, easier questions don't make these pupils feel safer; they simply increase the fear. Such pupils are most happy to venture a contribution when they are pretty sure that no-one else knows the answer either.

The fear of making a mistake will reduce the learning potential of your question-asking. Many studies have found that students' willingness to take risks in class reduces as they get older.

So what strategies will help you to promote a supportive environment in which pupils offer suggestions and test ideas without fear?

Overcoming the fear

- Always thank pupils for their contribution
- Ask *'How can we find out?'* rather than *'What is the answer?'*
- Value mistakes – discuss their potential for learning
- Display currently unanswered questions, with an invitation to respond
- Use meaningful, real life scenarios to generate your questions
- Validate and respect pupil responses, perhaps list them or use sticky-notes
- Allow time – don't make your students feel rushed

- Model your own thought processes, particularly *'what if..'* situations
- Encourage pupils to ask questions
- Develop and use positive non-verbal responses
- Pose open questions often and point out the possibility of multiple answers
- Avoid *'guess what I'm thinking'* situations
- Respond to the reasoning behind the answer
- Discuss the explanatory potential and problem-solving contribution of answers
- Recognise and appreciate divergent and creative answers
- Avoid the use of *'right'* and *'wrong'* and *'good'* and *'bad'* in relation to answers when possible

Mistakes as learning opportunities

Interactive dialogue; feedback; the correction of mistakes, misunderstandings and weak constructs are key to providing both teacher and students with the information they need to build meaning and correct misunderstandings.

The teacher's questioning brings into play two 'feedback loops' – one to the teacher and one to the learner. It tells the teacher how many students have 'got it' so far, flags those who haven't (and suggests remedial action to be taken), and informs about the appropriateness of the pace and challenge presented so far.

It also tells students if they have got it, partly got it or not got it at all. They can then re-think, ask the teacher or a friend and re-construct their learning. (If they are alert, it also tells students how many of their classmates have or haven't got it – something else for the teacher to be aware of!)

If the teacher is to be able to correct misunderstandings, there needs to be a very high participation rate, followed by good teacher feedback and remedial action. This requires high-quality dialogue, between students, as well as between the teacher and the class.

The blame-free classroom

In his book *Evidence-Based Teaching*, Geoff Petty refers to the 'blame-free classroom', where making mistakes is seen as a part of the learning process. Learning is sometimes a process of trial and error and there is a sense of *'we (including the teacher) are all in this together'*.

Many schools and teachers prefer to keep class rules to a minimum, but if you are concerned about the questioning environment you may wish to introduce a set of explicit rules relating to whole-class question situations. As ever, the students should come up with the content. Here is an example from a year 9 class, based on Petty's 'towards a blame-free classroom' ground rules:

- Respect your classmates' efforts. Never take the mickey if someone gets something wrong
- Be brave – try out your ideas
- If you don't understand – say so
- We all make mistakes. That's how we learn
- Don't worry if you don't understand first time – ask!
- The one who says the mistake is not the only one who thought it

Climate control

It is essential that you get the climate right if your pupils are to take risks and maximise their learning.

Encourage	**Discourage**
Mutual support	Competition
Partly-formed answers	*'I don't know'*
Exploration of wrong answers	Ridicule
Discussion	Single question followed by single answer
Thinking time	Throw-away answers
Explanation	Rote learning
Reference to prior comments	Isolated thinking

Participate! Conflicting social norms

If a colleague told you that a group of teachers from your school was going to learn Morris dancing and they would like you to join them, it would be perfectly acceptable for you to politely decline. If you travel on the bus or tube, you are probably not offended when your fellow passengers avoid eye contact. Indeed, you respect their space and privacy. In school, however, participation is expected. For teachers, the expectation that students will participate overrides the norms of respecting privacy and the right to non-engagement.

Some of your students may not understand this and others will dislike it. You may need to be very explicit about this expectation. You can weave it into the strategies you use – no hands up, mini whiteboards etc – but once it is clear that all students are expected to engage with the question, a paradox becomes apparent: the easiest way for a student to get a moment's peace is to participate!

Of course, there will be times when, for their own reasons, a particular student does need space and you will be sensitive to this, but, as a general rule, if you ask a question you are entitled to call on anyone to attempt an answer.

Pupil passivity

Is *'I don't know'* ever an acceptable answer?

You will have met disengaged pupils who resist answering questions, respond with a blunt, *'I don't know'* or use more subtle 'leave me alone' signals. Faced with this behaviour (day-in-day-out), sometimes we subconsciously accept that students have the right to be passive. It can be demotivating to the teacher and contagious amongst pupils.

'Pupil factors' for disengagement may be many and complex but might include:

- Overconfidence
- Language difficulties
- Lack of interest in the subject
- Peer pressure

- Lack of confidence
- Personal issues
- Lack of interest in education generally

Unless you want a herd of RHINOs (Really Here In Name Only), this attitude needs challenging.

Overcoming pupil passivity

In *Classroom Questioning 101*, U.S. educator Ivan Hannel describes seven principles and practices to overcome pupil passivity:

Principle	Practice
Learning is not optional	Involuntary questioning – all students may be asked the question, the keen or the reluctant
Under-trained, not under-brained	Equalise questioning – ask challenging questions of all your students, and ask all students equally
Stay in questioning mode	Allow 'Wait Time', refrain from telling, showing, explaining, hinting and helping
I want the reason, not the answer	Follow answers with a supplementary question. Ask why they think that, or ask another student to support or challenge
Stay positive	Keep questions neutral or positive in both tone and inquiry. Don't let divergence or poor answers drag you into negativity
Discourage guessing	Random guessing is of no use. Prediction and estimation, however, are to be encouraged
Overcoming 'I don't know'	The teacher's response is to ask at least one more, possibly two or three more questions of that student

The 'I don't know' attitude

Let's be clear about the *'I don't know'* statement. Yes, you want your students to be honest with you and tell you if they don't know something. That's not what this is about. This is about 'I don't know' as an attitude – it is not a *sufficient* answer. If you are prepared to allow the actual words *'I don't know'*, expect them to be followed immediately by hypothesising or at least wondering:

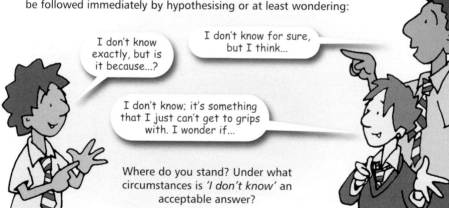

I don't know exactly, but is it because...?

I don't know for sure, but I think...

I don't know; it's something that I just can't get to grips with. I wonder if...

Where do you stand? Under what circumstances is *'I don't know'* an acceptable answer?

Practice makes…

A lot of pupils don't like to speak for an extended period in front of their peers about anything at all, let alone under the pressure of a questioning teacher.

Creating activities where students practise speaking in front of the class (reporting back on tasks, role play, etc) without the added anxiety of a question will ease this discomfort and allow pupils to concentrate on their thinking.

Speaking in pairs and working in small groups also provide opportunities for the less confident. Whole-class answering methods (see pages 89-91) can also ensure that the teacher sees what the 'shy' student is thinking in response to whole-class questioning, even if they are not answering verbally.

Do you know a student whose shyness is the only thing stopping them from answering whole-class questions? What can you do to build their confidence?

Equalising quality and quantity

Do you avoid asking the hardest questions of certain students? Why might that be? Perhaps you are conscious of the need to scaffold the learning, bearing in mind each student's zone of proximal development. Or it might be that you don't want to embarrass the student. (Perhaps you remember that happening to you when *you* were at school?)

Hannel suggests there is more to it than this. Could it be that when a student can't answer a question we feel that we have failed as teachers? That we want to hear correct, appropriate answers; not just for the student's benefit, but for ours too? The suggestion is that when teachers become focused on success they become averse to the risk of asking a difficult question of someone who may not provide an acceptable answer. Hannel's response is that in the context of questioning, it is *effort* that we should be striving for, not guaranteed success.

What do you think? Do you agree that most students' self-esteem (and yours) will withstand a tricky question if there's a supportive environment?

All aboard!

How many of your students automatically raise their hands when you ask a question? And how many of the rest are happy to let them, in the hope that you will go for the easy option and choose someone you're pretty sure will give a good answer?

In an ideal world of course, when you ask a question *all* your pupils will be thinking about an answer. (And creating a supportive, self-correcting climate will encourage that.) But even if they *are* all thinking, how do you know?

Strategies that increase the likelihood of everyone thinking	Strategies that show you *who* is thinking
Think, Pair, Share	Mini-whiteboards
No hands	Thumbs up
Lolly sticks or bingo balls	A, B, C, D, E cards

Is there anyone in your class who you suspect is getting away with not engaging with your questions? Try one of these strategies which are all described in detail later in this book in the section entitled 'Delivering the Question'.

Mind your language

How you speak to your pupils is vitally important. The language you use influences the outcomes you get. For instance:

1. Encourage divergent thinking

- *'What is...'; 'How does...'; 'Where are...'* all suggest a single correct answer
- *'What might / could be...' 'How might...' 'Where could....' 'To what extent...'* suggest that there are many possible answers. By slightly rephrasing your question you can encourage divergent thinking

2. Neutral response

- A neutral response to pupils' comments encourages further responses
- Over-blown and enthusiastic praise makes other students less likely to contribute further
- Negative responses reduce tentative 'thinking out loud' comments

How do you balance the need to support students' self-esteem with the idea of making neutral responses to their comments?

Praise effort, not ability

Carol Dweck's work* on student motivation divides pupils into two types, dependent on their beliefs about their own ability:

Fixed mindset students	Growth mindset students
Believe intelligence is static, genetic	Believe intelligence can be developed
Gain motivation from appearing clever	Gain motivation from learning
Avoid challenge	Relish challenge
Give up	Persevere
Ignore or devalue criticism	Learn from criticism
Feel threatened by others' success	Gain inspiration and learn from others' success
May plateau early and underachieve	Likely to continue extending achievement

Whether your students adopt a fixed or growth mindset can be influenced by the way you respond to their answers.

(You can find out more about Carol Dweck's mindset work at http://mindsetonline.com)

Praise effort, not ability

'Well done Sue, you're good at this aren't you?'

Responses that praise people for 'being clever' lead to a fixed mindset, resulting in decreasing motivation and a lack of resilience. They lead students to believe that:
- Success is due to innate attributes
- Difficulties are personal weakness

'Yes, that was good thinking Suhaib; well done for following the idea through.'

Reponses that praise effort, involvement, perseverance and learning lead to a growth mindset and increased motivation. They lead students to believe that:
- Esteem comes from effort and the use of effective strategies
- Errors and misunderstandings are a learning opportunity
- Everyone can earn praise

The problem with praise

In their 1998 review of formative assessment, Black and Wiliam compare judgemental with informative feedback. The principles they outline relate to all 'assessment for learning' strategies, but many are relevant to questioning practices:

Judgemental feedback – characteristics	Informative feedback - characteristics
Encourages competition	Refers to assessment criteria
Compares students	Gives pointers for improvement
Students protective of self-esteem	Students feel effort is recognised and valued
Avoid risk and challenge, develop complacency	Commitment and emotional involvement rise
Extrinsic motivation, teacher driven, shallow learning	Intrinsic motivation, value driven, deep learning
Seek praise rather than learning	Seek understanding
Right answer syndrome	Esteem from effort, so more likely to take risks
Success is key, mistakes are shameful	Learning comes from effort and practice
Need to put in effort is an admission of stupidity	Mistakes are useful informative feedback
Performance and effort are reward-led	Learning is an end in itself

(Table adapted from Extremes of Summative versus Informative Feedback, Petty p97)

Do you see the connection between this and Dweck's 'fixed' versus 'growth' mindset ideas? Which of these characteristics ring true for the students you currently teach?

Review

This chapter has shown how the way you ask questions and respond to students' answers sets the tone in your class, influences the students' mind-sets and contributes to the overall learning culture. It has looked at strategies for maximising engagement and considered the unwilling and the shy.

- Which idea in this chapter most makes you stop and think about your own practice?

- Are there any ideas you can develop to enhance the questioning environment in your class?

- Which could make a difference fairly soon and which would need a longer time scale to show an effect?

Raising
Questions

 The Questioning
Environment

 Framing
Questions

 Delivering
the Question

 Responding to
the Answer

 Improving
Your Practice

Framing
Questions

Which question?

When constructing your question a series of decisions has to be made:

1. What is the question ABOUT?
- What learning objective does it address?
- How does it connect to prior knowledge?

2. What is the question FOR?
- Developing concepts
- Engaging
- Activating prior knowledge
- Formative assessment
- Probing
- Scaffolding
- Inference / interpretation
- Transfer
- Reflection

3. At what LEVEL is the question to be pitched?
- Select a taxonomy
- Identify the appropriate level

4. In what CONTEXT will the question be asked?
- Individual
- Pairs
- Small groups
- Whole class

5. HOW will you phrase the question?
- Who, what, where, when, how....?
- Fact first question
- Context-setting statement + question

6. Is this one of a SERIES?
- If so, return to 1

Clarity through planning

To get as many pupils as possible to engage with your questions you need to make sure that they all understand what you are asking. Complex conceptual questions can still be asked in clear language – 'low access, high challenge'.

Clear questions tend to be:

| Succinct | Direct | Context bound | Precise | Solitary |

Planning your key questions in advance helps – it's easy to ask a badly-phrased question in the heat of the moment.

Poorly-phrased questions tend to be:

| Wordy | Ambiguous | Cloaked in additional information |

| Grammatically incorrect |

'Where a river flows into the sea is called what?' may be understandable, but it is clumsy and adds an extra layer of processing.

That last question should have been phrased how?

Using key questions

Key questions get to the heart of a concept and relate directly to the learning outcome for the lesson. A feature of a good key question is that it looks forward, even when being used evaluatively; it creates a sense of 'what's next?' For example:

- *Why are some people rich and some people poor?*
- *What happens when you think?*

Key questions may be used at the start of the lesson to stimulate interest and enquiry, during the lesson, or at the end to summarise what has been learned. There may be one or more for a lesson. Usually they are planned, but sometimes they present themselves serendipitously.

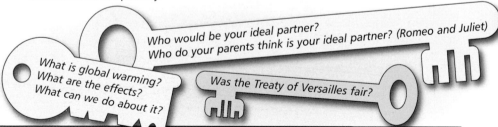

Who would be your ideal partner?
Who do your parents think is your ideal partner? (Romeo and Juliet)

What is global warming?
What are the effects?
What can we do about it?

Was the Treaty of Versailles fair?

Sequencing questions

Pupils' responses will improve if you prepare a series of clearly and logically connected questions that move thinking forward and upward. You can't jump straight to higher order questions in the abstract. You need some knowledge to base your higher order thinking on. Try asking someone who doesn't know what a metaphor is:

> 'In what ways do metaphors help, and in what way do they hinder, our understanding of the world?'

There are many sequencing patterns. Two of the most effective – **extending and lifting**, and **narrow to broad** – are explained on the next pages.

Extending and lifting

First, you ask a number of extending questions on the same cognitive level, before lifting the questions to the next level. For example:

Extending questions to focus and set the context:
Who is Holden Caulfield?
Where is Holden as he narrates the story?
Why wasn't Holden at the big football game?
Why wouldn't Holden be back to Pencey after the Christmas vacation?

And the lifting question that takes your students' thinking to the next level:
How does J.D. Salinger's using Holden as the narrator affect our understanding of the events?

Narrow to broad

This pattern involves gradually increasing the cognitive level as the sequence progresses. In this pattern you start with lower level, specific questions and move to higher level, general questions. (You might use Bloom's taxonomy.) For example:

1. Narrow / lower order

What were Mr Tom's home and village like?

Why is Tom so grumpy and lonely?

2. Broadening / mid order

What did you learn about relationships between children and adults from the story?

3. Broad / higher order

Tom helps William. How does William help Tom?

Why should Tom be allowed to adopt William?

What sort of adult do you think William would grow up to be?

How might William have been different if he had never met Tom?

Open and closed; fishing and shooting

The most basic distinction between questions is **open** and **closed**.

Closed questions have a single correct answer, eg yes / no, a date, a name. An important characteristic of closed questions is that control of the conversation stays with the questioner. They can feel safe and keep the lesson moving.

Open questions have no single correct answer, many possibilities, are sometimes a matter of opinion or interpretation. Open questions more often than not lead towards higher order thinking.

Thinking skills guru Edward de Bono uses a hunting metaphor to describe questions:

- **Fishing questions** (open) – you cast your net out to see what you will catch
- **Shooting questions** (closed) – you have a particular target in your sights

These questions are sometimes referred to as 'broad or narrow' and children respond well to the idea of 'fat' and 'skinny' questions.

Open and closed questions

Closed questions have their place when seeking facts or information. They provide the foundations on which higher order thinking is built.

A mixture of closed and open questions is most effective for pupils of all ages. From around age 10 and upwards, students benefit from roughly equal amounts of open and closed questions. In practice, that means that most teachers should try to ask more open questions.

A closed question can be opened by:

- Adding '....and why' or '...and how do you know?'
- Refocusing from the specific to the general, eg *'Was Picasso feeling sad when he painted this?'* becomes *'To what extent does this picture convey the mood of the artist?'* and onward to, *'How can mood be represented visually?'*

Do you know what proportion of your questions are open questions?

Open and closed questions in maths

In case you got the idea that maths was missing the fun of open questions, try these:

Closed	Open
3 + ? = 7 7 − 3 = ?	What is the same and what is different about addition and subtraction?
What is 7 + 11?	How do you add 11? Why do 7 + 11 and 11 + 7 give the same answer?
What do the interior angles in a triangle add up to?	How do you explain why the interior angles in any triangle add up to 180?
What shape is this?	How do we know that this is a square?

Opening possibilities

We have seen that when asking open questions it is important to signal that you are not looking for a single right answer. You can do this by subtly rephrasing questions. In many cases swapping the word *'is'* for *'could be'* or *'might be'* does the trick.

- *'Why?'* can become *'in what ways?'*
  Why is evidence important to scientists?
  In what ways is evidence important to scientists?
- Opening the sentence with, *'What is your understanding of...?; Can you think of different ways to...?; To what extent might....?'* gives the message that you are open to more than a single correct answer

Can I?

'Can I go to the toilet?'

'I don't know, can you?'

I'm sure you have heard a variation on this cliché. As teachers we sometimes fall into the same trap:

'Can you tell me...?'
'Do you know...?'

Questions like this are, strictly speaking, closed questions: an appropriate answer would be *'Yes'* or *'No'*.

While most students will interpret the question and give an answer along the lines you were hoping for, it is not setting a good example. Such questions can be confusing for pupils in the early stages of learning English or who are on the autistic spectrum and may interpret your words literally.

The 5Ws (and H)

Who? **W**hat? **W**here? **W**hen? **W**hy? **H**ow?

Sometimes factual information needs to be established before higher order thinking can begin. The 5Ws and H, much relied on in factual accounts, provide a good checklist when establishing that the lower order foundations are laid firmly.
A series of 5Ws and H can prepare the class for deeper thinking.

Take this example from a World War II History lesson:

1 *What was the evacuation?*   4 *Why?*

2 *When did it happen?*   5 *Where were they evacuated to?*

3 *Who was evacuated?*   6 *How did they get there?*

On the face of it, the 5 Ws and H all lead to closed questions even though none can be answered with yes or no. If we use *'might'* or *'could'* to follow the opening words, possibilities and opinion come into the discussion:

- Why might a parent not want to send their child away?

- What good things could happen to the evacuees, even if they were unhappy?

Hinge questions

A hinge question is designed to tell you what pupils know about a crucial concept. The outcome of asking the question determines the direction of the rest of the lesson.

Hinge questions should be asked around half way through the lesson. You need to know what every student thinks, so choose one of the all-student response systems described in the next section. You must be able to collect and interpret the responses from all the students. What happens next depends on the answers you get.

This seems like a sound idea and straightforward enough until you try to write the question. It needs to capture possible misconceptions as well as right and wrong answers. It needs to tell you about the pupils' thinking. Of course the hinge question can be followed up with probing and exploring as shown later in the book, but its purpose is to give you as much information as possible as efficiently as possible.

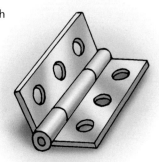

Tip: Offer more than one correct answer.

Example hinge questions

Which of these would increase the temperature of boiling water?

1. Adding more heat.
2. Adding more water.
3. You can't increase the temperature of boiling water.
4. Adding salt.

A rhombus is:

1. A 2-D shape with two pairs of parallel sides.
2. A quadrilateral with two pairs of parallel sides, each side being of equal length.
3. A quadrilateral where all four sides have equal length. Opposite sides are parallel and opposite angles are equal.
4. A quadrilateral where all four sides have equal length. Opposite sides are parallel and all angles are right angles.

Answers:
1. Incorrect
2. Incorrect
3. Incorrect
4. Correct

Answers:
1. Correct but incomplete
2. Correct but incomplete
3. Correct
4. Incorrect

Get emotional

> 'All learning has an emotional base' (**Plato**)

We learn best when our emotions are engaged. If you can engage your students' emotions you are creating a direct link to their motivation. Emotional connections help learners stay engaged, create meaning and commit material to memory.

How can we use questioning to engage emotion? By asking questions that require students to empathise:

'What would you have done?'
'How would you feel if…?'
'How would you respond if it was our community…?'

Use 'you' and 'we' when you construct a question to personalise the context and make the pupils see that this is about them.

Make use of puzzlement, mystery, fear, joy and wonder in your questions.

Use thinking words

Don't shy away from technical vocabulary with younger children. They often surprise with their metacognitive abilities, and will certainly respond to the idea of fat and skinny questions, or open and closed. The terms *'same'*, *'similar'*, *'different'*, *'compare'* and *'contrast'* are key to their development.

If you are teaching older children, make sure that they know the meaning of:

Many students think that they are synonymous and mean *'tell me about…'*
At the appropriate stage, make sure that your students are aware of both the general and subject-specific uses of *'evaluate'*, ie:

- General – make a judgement based on agreed criteria
- Mathematical – determine the value of

Analogy – same but different

Questions that ask pupils to identify similarities and differences between two or more concepts aim straight at higher order thinking and are highly effective in activating the cognitive system. Connections are made, patterns seen, and comparisons and contrasts identified. Try using analogies, ie:

- Explaining something unknown in terms of something known
- Explaining something unseen in terms of something seen
- Explaining something unfamiliar in terms of something familiar

Ask your pupils to develop their own analogies. Young learners need explicit help with this, but by overt modelling you'll soon show how they work. Self-created analogies (as long as they are accurate) are more effective. A useful question to ask is *'How far is this analogy correct?'*

Examples

- In History many pupils will make an analogy between conflict in the global arena and playground behaviour

- In Year 2 Music pupils offered: *'Moving by step is like walking up or down stairs' 'Glissando is like sliding down a slide'*

Analogy examples

There are many ways to use analogy. You could:

- Use a comparison table to answer the question:
  What are the similarities and differences between the human eye and a camera?
- Use a Venn diagram to demonstrate:
  How is the brain like a muscle? How are they different?
- Ask questions about the analogy and then ask pupils to translate this into reality:
  If 'All the world's a stage', who are the actors?
- Ask questions about the reality, but get students to refer to the analogy in their answer: *What does a good story opening do that a 'hors d'oeuvre' does?*

Caution – No analogy is perfect and invalid comparisons can sometimes lead to misunderstanding. If young children think of electricity 'flowing' like water, this is not going to help when studying advanced physics.

Fact First

Fact First questions are good for checking that knowledge (memory) translates into understanding. Here's how to use them:

1. Take a fact question
- *What is a Local Area Network?*
- *Who is known as 'the father of medicine'?*
- *Who are the 'Stolen Generations'?*

2. Turn it into a statement
- A Local Area Network (LAN) is a computer network linking devices within a building or group of adjacent buildings
- Hippocrates was known as 'the father of medicine'
- The 'Stolen Generations' are the Australian Aboriginal children taken away from their families to be brought up in institutions or fostered out to white families

3. Create a new question
- A Local Area Network (LAN) is a computer network linking devices within a building or group of adjacent buildings. What might be the benefits of a LAN for a small organisation using fewer than five computers?
- Why is Hippocrates known as 'the father of medicine'?
- The 'Stolen Generations' are the Australian Aboriginal children taken away from their families. Why did the people who organised this think it was a good idea?

Big questions

Include 'big' questions in your teaching to stimulate curiosity and a spirit of enquiry. Big questions are the significant questions that get to the heart and essence of a topic. They can be current or enduring. They can uncover things we take for granted and raise awareness. They enable us to question values, beliefs and prejudices. Each subject will have its own and there are abundant cross-curricular concepts to be discussed.

- *Where does creativity come from?*
- *What does it mean to be successful?*
- *What is art for?*
- *Why are there so many different types of insect?*
- *Are justice and the law the same thing?*
- *Should life be fair?*
- *How do you know the person next to you is alive?*

Spend some time on the big questions regularly and your students will start asking the questions too.

Rhetorical questions

Rhetorical questions are not really questions at all – they are statements masquerading as questions. They are usually not meant to be answered; if they are, the intention is usually that the students agree with the teacher.

- *Why do I bother?*
- *How many times do I have to tell you?*
- *What's the matter with you?*
- *Am I talking to myself?*
- *What time do you call this?*
- *Did I tell you it was going to be easy?*
- *Look at Janet's picture. Isn't it clever the way she's captured the reflection?*

Notice that it's quite hard to find examples of positive rhetorical questions. As teachers, we should avoid them, shouldn't we?

Thinking hats

Although Edward de Bono's well known *Six Thinking Hats* is essentially a problem-solving tool, the coloured hats can be used as prompts to create a series of teacher questions.

Hat colour	Mode of thinking	Question prompt
White	Facts	*What do you know about...?*
Red	Emotion	*What do you feel about...?*
Green	Creative	*What new ideas can you think of /about...?*
Yellow	Positive	*What are the good things about...?*
Black	Cautious	*What do we need to be careful about...?*
Blue	Process thinking	*How should we go about this...?*

Fermi questions

Enrico Fermi was a physicist renowned for his creativity. He challenged his students to use estimation and common sense reasoning to calculate quantities that were difficult or impossible to measure. Fermi questions are a good way of demonstrating that how you think about a problem is more important than the answer. For our purposes, we're looking for a formula, rather than a quantity as the answer.

Examples
- *How many ping pong balls would it take to fill the school hall?*
- *How many bricks make our school?*
- *How high are a million kids standing on each other's shoulders?*
- *How long would it take to count to a million?*
- *How many hairs are there on a human head?*
- *How many jelly beans fill a one-litre jar?*
- *What is the mass in kilograms of all the pupils in your school?*
- *If it were possible to walk from here to the moon, how many years would it take?*
- *How much has the mass of the human population increased in the last year?*
- *How many swimming strokes would it take to swim from England to France?*
- *If a pea represents the earth, what could represent the sun, and how far away would it be to maintain scale?*

> Search the internet for Fermi questions to find many, many more.

Fermi questions – example

How much human blood is there in the world? (Year 3, 4 and 5 pupils in SE London.)

The number of people in the world, multiplied by how much blood a person has

But not everyone's the same size

Do some people have less blood than others?

What about someone with one arm or leg?

How much blood is waiting to be used?

How many accidents are there where blood is lost?

Do dead people still have blood?

Is there anyone in the space station at the moment? If there is we'd have to subtract their blood from the total.

The final decision

The amount of human blood in the world = **a x b + c + d – (b x e)**

a = the number of people in the world, living and recently deceased
b = the average amount of blood in a human (allowing for babies and amputees etc)
c = the amount of blood stored in blood banks and blood tests
d = the average amount of blood spilt through accidents/nosebleeds in five minutes
e = the number of astronauts in space

Pitfalls in framing questions

We have now looked at a wide range of strategies for framing questions clearly, appropriately and to make the best use of assessment and feedback opportunities.

Here is a quick checklist of the most common errors:

- Too many lower order questions
- Unclear phrasing, grammar or word choice
- Making the questions impersonal – use 'you' and 'we'
- Questions not related to each other
- Asking too many of the same type of question
- Not pitching the question accurately
- Be careful with rhetorical questions

Raising
Questions

 The Questioning
Environment

 Framing
Questions

 Delivering
the Question

 Responding to
the Answer

 Improving
Your Practice

Delivering
the Question

It ain't what you do...

Having carefully crafted your questions, and confident now in your ability to spontaneously create others, the next step is to present them in the best way possible. How will you deliver your killer questions? This section looks at delivery techniques that maximise your questions' effectiveness.

Did everyone catch that?

Irrespective of the particular techniques you use, if you deliver your questions with genuine curiosity and enthusiasm, you will be modelling the behaviours you are seeking to foster and drawing the learners in.

The speed at which you ask your questions is important:

Adult speech rate	5-7 year olds' processing speed	13-16 year olds' processing speed
170 words per minute	120 words per minute	140-145 words per minute

How fast do you think you speak when asking the class a question?

Do you see what I'm asking?

What's the difference between hearing a question and reading a question?

While it is important to develop your pupils' listening skills, sometimes it is appropriate to display a question visually, particularly if it is complex and / or is key to the development of the lesson.

Imagine yourself as a pupil (or as a teacher on a training course). A question is asked about a complex idea which you are told to spend a minute thinking about. Would it benefit you to have the question displayed in written form?

As well as avoiding the *'What was the question?'* response, the visible question means that all the brain-power can be directed to thinking about the content of the question without having to remember it.

Where a dialogue produces a question that needs to be followed up later, this can be written on a sticky-note and parked on your Thinking Wall. If a question forms the basis of further enquiry it needs to be presented more permanently.

Not just *what*, but *when*?

As well as the complexities of *what* you ask, there is the matter of when you ask it.

Reading research studies (see page 125) have shown that, in general terms, lower ability and younger children respond better to questions that are presented *after* they have had some time to investigate the material. By contrast, with more able children it is helpful to ask questions *before* looking at the material so that they can read with a particular focus in mind. (It's a similar process to telling pupils sitting a written exam to read the question before looking at the comprehension passage.)

Think about whether it would be useful to vary the timing of your questions – before or after the stimulus. Each situation will have its own benefits; don't get stuck in a rut.

 Read poem ▶ ask questions

 'We're going to read a poem and I'd like you to look out for examples of x and y.'

Eye to eye...

When asking a whole-class question, it is important that you scan the class as a way of reinforcing the notion that *anyone* may be asked to answer. We've all come across pupils who try to avoid eye contact in the hope of not being chosen to answer.

There's even a Facebook page, *'Deliberately avoiding eye contact with the teacher so they won't pick you'*.

Once a student has been chosen, how much continuous eye contact do you give and expect in return? In western culture eye contact is seen as showing attentiveness. Looking someone in the eye is said to suggest truthfulness.

However, making optimum eye contact with students is a delicate balance: many will find a determined glare uncomfortable and concentration-breaking. Too much looking = staring. And as we all know, it's rude to stare.

There are, in fact, some good reasons for not insisting on constant eye contact.

...or not eye to eye

- In many cultures eye contact is seen as disrespectful or rude. A lack of eye contact could be a sign of respect

- The amount of information being processed when looking at a human face is enough to stop some students giving their best answer. Individuals who are thinking – lower or higher order – tend to avert eye gaze. Not looking at you when answering could be a good sign

- Many (but by no means all) pupils with Asperger syndrome find eye contact difficult and will not be able to answer and hold your gaze

Try discussing eye contact with your pupils. They will know the difference between looking upwards when thinking, and gazing distractedly out of the window. They will know the pressure of 'all eyes on you' when answering a question. It's all part of the learning conversation.

Wait Time 1 – the miracle pause

Your pupils need thinking time, particularly if you're expecting higher order thinking, an opinion or an emotional response. Consistent use of 'Wait Time' (sometimes called 'think time') ensures that time to think is built in to your class structure.

Direct the question to the class		Wait for at least three to five seconds		Name a pupil to respond

This is often described as **'Pose, Pause, Pounce'**. It's a strategy that:
- Encourages participation from all learners
- Reduces *'I don't know'* answers
- Builds students' confidence and reduces anxiety
- Increases engagement
- Encourages longer, richer answers
- Improves the logical consistency of students' explanations
- Increases the use of evidence to support inferences
- Increases unsolicited, relevant contributions
- Increases the number of speculative responses

Still waiting

So what is the optimum period for Wait Time 1?

Three to five seconds is generally agreed to be the minimum. Three seconds is the point at which positive things start to happen. Far more than five seconds is often appropriate – it depends on the cognitive level of the question. Use your judgement.

You may find the long pause difficult to sustain. Initially it can feel uncomfortable, both for you and your students. You may sometimes expect to see tumbleweed blowing across the classroom. Keep at it – increase the pause little by little. A signal from you, eg a raised hand, or pointing to your head can be used to indicate 'thinking time'. Talk with your class about the question and answer process. Explain that:

- Thinking is a time-consuming activity
- Thinking time should be quiet time
- During the pause they should be thinking about their answer
- They should be ready to answer so the whole class can hear
- If another pupil is called on they should listen to that answer and compare theirs
- They should respect thinking time for others, even if they are quick to formulate an answer

I'm thinking

> Katherine (Y5) is gazing into space.
> Teacher: *'What are you doing Katherine?'*
> Katherine: *'Thinking.'*
> Teacher: *'Well stop thinking and get on with your work.'*

Answering questions takes thinking time, confidence and security. It is a multi-step process that runs like this:

- Pay attention to the question
- Move the question into working memory and make sense of it
- Search long-term memory for relevant information
- Match information in long-term memory and bring into working memory
- Think through the question
- Generate possible answers
- Select most appropriate answer(s)

It's no wonder that Wait Time 1 is effective!

Internal and external processors

Experience and research tell us that different people's thinking processes work at different speeds and in different ways.

Have you noticed how some people (adults and children alike) talk through their answers – thinking aloud – until they sort their thoughts? They are **external processors** and need to hear what they are thinking, correcting themselves as they go along. They will need time to express themselves.

Others prefer to mull their thoughts over and craft an answer before saying anything out loud. These **internal processors** will require more quiet time before they speak.

Talk about this with your pupils when you are stressing the importance of giving people time to think. Neither is 'right' or 'best', it's a personal preference.

Which are you? Can you think of pupils who fit into each category? Is there an implication for how you set up thinking partners in 'Think, Pair, Share' activities? (pages 83-85)

Look no hands!

Do you find the same few children answering your questions? And some who never put up their hand?

'No hands up' has become a well-used strategy. It takes time for teachers and pupils to break well-established habits, but is worth the effort. You ask a question; no-one is to put their hand up, but everyone should be thinking of an answer, because you could choose anyone. The possibility of being 'chosen' may freeze some pupils' ability to think, but over time, and within a no-blame culture, they will come to relax and contribute.

Who to choose? Any form of random selection will work – bingo style **ping pong balls** or **lolly sticks** with pupils' names on (also known as 'equity sticks'); **IT name-generators** (Powerpoint is useful in that you can use pupils' pictures or their own page design); or **spreadsheet software** offers a more clinical option. Instructions for the latter two are readily found on the web.

Tips:
- Don't let the pupil selection system overshadow the question itself
- If using lolly sticks or ping-pong balls check once in a while that they're all still there!

Pose, pause, pounce, bounce – basketball not table tennis

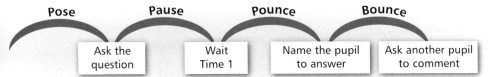

Pose — Ask the question

Pause — Wait Time 1

Pounce — Name the pupil to answer

Bounce — Ask another pupil to comment

Table tennis. Traditional teacher questioning uses the Initiation / Response / Evaluation communication pattern (IRE). The teacher asks a question to find out whether the student(s) know the answer. The student answer is evaluated by the teacher who makes a brief reply – *'yes, good'*, etc. The interaction ends and the lesson moves on. IRE has its place, checking for factual knowledge or recall, but it doesn't contribute much to the development of understanding and of thinking.

Basketball. If, instead of evaluating the student's response, you make a neutral comment and invite another student to participate, you are using the Initiation / Response / Follow-up communication pattern (IRF). Sustained IRF turns the interaction into a dialogue. As students gain experience and understand your expectations, your input can be minimised.

Basketball follow-ups

Possible follow-up prompts to encourage basketball dialogue:

'Thank you Alice. George – do you agree or disagree with Alice? Why?'

'Is that completely right?'

'Tracy, could Daisy's answer be more accurate?'

'Mike, what did you think of that answer?'

'Faisal, how would you explain Gill's answer to a younger pupil?'

'Does anyone want to add anything?'

'Can anyone add a little more?'

This approach encourages thinking out loud and the exploration of half-formed ideas as the class works together to build answers, extending breadth and depth.

Think, Pair, Share

Having carefully crafted your killer question, you might like to use 'Think, Pair, Share' (TPS) – to ensure that you get maximum engagement.

Think   Each pupil thinks for a minute about their own ideas (no talking)
Pair   In pairs, pupils compare their ideas, discuss and agree on an answer
Share   Joint ideas are shared with the whole class

- The THINK stage encourages all learners to become actively involved and increases the quality of response
- TPS supports connection-making and retention
- Pupils may be more willing to participate, since they can try out ideas with a partner, rather than in front of the class
- Thinking aloud helps to make sense of new ideas
- The pair's combined idea is likely to be superior to the individual's
- Easy to use, even in large classes

Think, Pair, Share – hints and tips

- Assign partners – ability, mixed ability, gender… you decide. *'Turn to the person next to you'* can work if the seating is set up that way, but don't let partner-choosing take over from the purpose of the activity

- Change partners – half-termly perhaps. Each pairing type has its advantages

- Make sure you allow enough **THINK** time – students could give a thumbs-up when they are ready to share with their partner

- Monitor the **PAIR** discussions – listen out for misunderstandings and exemplar comments to call on

- If you notice that one partner dominates – divide the **PAIR** stage into three sections; Partner A speaks first, Partner B second, followed by discussion

- Monitor who **SHARES** – encourage turn-taking in the whole-class feedback

- Sometimes use a graphic organiser – brief notes or diagrams, like the example on the next page, suffice – it can help learners to retain ideas, and encourage partners to listen to each other

- With complex issues you might sometimes like to use Think, Pair, Switch, Share – after the initial paired discussion new pairs are made and the discussion continues.

Think, Pair, Share – hints and tips

Think, Pair, Share

My name

My partner's name

Question/ problem	My Ideas	My partner's ideas	What we want to share

Focusing them on the type of question

Talk with your pupils about question types. Use appropriate terminology for their age – *'fat and skinny questions'; 'open and closed'; 'convergent and divergent'.*

Alert the class when you are changing question type – it allows them to be ready for a different style of thinking and prepares them for an appropriate mode of answer.

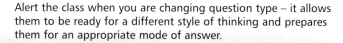

'I've asked you some convergent questions and we've remembered who were the main characters, what they did and when. I'm now going to ask you to use a different kind of thinking by asking some divergent questions. If you had been in that situation... ...'

Telegraphing

Telegraphing a question is announcing the question but postponing the opportunity to answer. Pupils will have time to think about a response, either consciously or subconsciously, and the answers will be richer. You could:

- Tell the class that near the end of this lesson you will ask their opinion about…
- Have a question written on the board at the outset, but not refer to it until later
- Tell the class, *'Next lesson, I'm going to ask you…'*
- Last thing on Friday ask, *'Why do you think that… …happens? We'll talk about it next time I see you.'*
- Have a 'Question of the Week' posted on Monday, and addressed on Friday afternoon

Class brainstorm

The class brainstorm is a way of pooling ideas, modelling that there are no wrong answers. Ask your class a fat question, something that requires divergent thinking.

- *What if the 'cultural revolution' had never happened?*
- *How should we influence states with poor human rights records?*
- *What qualities would you look for when choosing the captain of a football team?*

Collate the answers on a whiteboard, grouping obviously related ideas together. Encourage responses from everyone and make clear that the purpose is to generate as many ideas as possible. Quirky and unusual are to be encouraged. (Think, Pair, Share or 'buzz groups' (page 92) can be used to generate and test initial ideas.)

Judgement is withheld at this stage – but ideas can be added to, adapted and built on. Make sure no-one criticises or evaluates at this stage. Look at things from new angles, challenge assumptions. Once the brainstorming has run its course, ask the class to identify ideas that link or connect. Look for overlaps and the potential for one idea to add to another. Draw out contradictory or opposite ideas.

Tip: If you have a class member who tends to dominate, give them the role of scribe.

All-student response systems

Thumbs

You want to be as sure as you can be that everyone is thinking when you ask a question. What better, then, than systems which show you every pupil's answer? These three pages suggest some all-student response systems, from the embodiment of simplicity to interactive technology.

When you ask the class a question you are delivering it to everyone, not just the pupil who is eventually chosen to speak.

Once you have an answer, ask the class to put their **thumbs up** if they agree, **thumbs down** if they disagree and **horizontal** if they are not sure. This gives you important information about current knowledge or opinions and a clue about who to choose next.

Mini whiteboards

Mini whiteboards – A5 size, with a dry-wipe marker and cloth for each pupil, kept in sets on their tables – are brilliant for even the youngest pupils but also highly effective at 'A level'.

Ask a question of the whole class. Everyone puts an answer on the mini whiteboard and turns the board to show you. Instant!

Ask a 'list' question – pupils make their list, then pair up and share lists. Each pupil ticks anything their partner had too and adds anything they missed.

With everyone in the class showing you a response, you can make comparisons: *'I can see that Joel has put the apostrophe between the 'c' and the 's', but Owen has put it after the 's'* – and create a whole-class dialogue based on knowing everyone's answer.

Multiple choice

For interactive, whole-class strategies, multiple choice is a quick way to see where your pupils are. Use small whiteboards, A to E cards, fingers held up or an electronic voting system. Make sure everyone has chosen an answer before asking all to reveal their choice at the same time.

Examples

Which word best describes a large object orbiting a star?

a) Sun

b) Solar system

c) Galaxy

d) Moon

e) Planet

Which of the following is true?

a) All plant cells contain chloroplasts

b) Most cells have a nucleus

c) Cellulose is used as a structural molecule in animals

d) All cells have a cell wall

e) Some cells contain cytoplasm

Note with multi-choice questions it is possible to have more than one correct answer.

Buzz groups

Arrange pupils in small groups to answer a big question or suggest solutions to a problem.

- *How would your life be different if you had one eye at the front of your head and one at the back?*
- *To what extent should you trust what you read on the internet?*
- *Under what circumstances is it ok to tell a lie?*
- *What might be the consequence of all the bees in the world dying?*

Eavesdrop on as many groups as possible in order to fuel follow-up questions about the process as well as the answer.

You then ask each group to contribute an answer. Either a volunteer in each group answers; you choose which individual in each group will answer; or if you give each group member a number before the discussion starts, you can select a 'number' to answer. This helps ensure maximum participation.

Pair checking

The teacher asks a question and students work on their own to find an answer. This could be something closed, such as a maths calculation or punctuation problem, or open, such as identifying as many ways as possible to …

Pupils then work with a partner, comparing answers, identifying positive points and suggesting improvements. The teacher asks for answers from a sample, the number depending on the possible range of responses.

Assertive questioning

Assertive questioning is a powerful whole-class interactive technique. Pupils construct their own meaning and sense; the teacher checks understanding and, if necessary, makes corrections.

1. Set up small groups – four or five pupils.
2. Ask a thought-provoking question, eg *'Is a flame alive?'* and tell the groups they are to produce a fully justified answer.
3. Monitor the reasoning – push for deep thinking.
4. Check that everyone has an answer, *'Hands up if you need two minutes more'*.
5. Nominate a pupil from each group in turn to explain the group's answer. Ask questions about the thinking behind the answer and the process. Thank the student, record the answer on the board but do not evaluate.

6. Point out, or ask pupils to identify inconsistencies between answers.
7. The class now considers and discusses all the answers and tries to come to a consensus. You might begin with a show of hands: *'Who agrees with…'* The aim is to come up with a class answer.
8. Only when the class has agreed an answer or answers do you make any comment about the merits of the answer. Make sure that you explain your own reasoning clearly.
9. Praise the pupils' work, particularly any examples of 'good thinking'.

Assertive questioning makes learners create their own meaning (remember constructivism on pages 10 and 11), stimulates curiosity and contributes to the development of the self-correcting classroom.

With high levels of pupil participation, dialogue, feedback and thinking time, this way of working ticks many boxes. And withholding the answer can be great fun for you as well as the pupils!

Bad habits

Don't ask too many questions at once
'What is the earthworm's place in the food chain and what would happen if they vanished overnight?' will confuse and distract. Which part of the question to address first? Thinking clearly about one part of the question will be hampered by trying to remember the other.

Don't answer your own question
Instead, use focus questioning (page 115) to establish the cause of the roadblock and enable you to scaffold a series of questions to lead the thinking in the required direction.

Don't ask a question and then repeat it, or rephrase it
Students will learn that they don't have to listen carefully first time, because you will repeat yourself. They will learn that they don't have to engage with intellectually challenging questions because you will paraphrase.

Raising Questions

 The Questioning Environment

 Framing Questions

 Delivering the Question

 Responding to the Answer

 Improving Your Practice

Responding to the Answer

Feedback, ethos, understanding...
in your hands

The response you make to a pupil's answer is a vital part of the lesson. It sets the tone of the lesson. It says to the pupils *I will take you and your answer seriously*. Your enthusiasm and interest (or ambivalence or boredom) send a clear signal to your class.

You need to practise *active* listening.

Your response to an answer also plays a part in the structure of the lesson. Is this an opportunity to investigate the material in depth, to seriously address misconceptions, or will you skate over the answer and continue with what you were going to do anyway?

Feedback

Feedback, particularly immediate, specific feedback, has more impact on students' learning than any other general teaching strategy*. Questioning is extremely potent here, since it is instant and continuous.

In practice, however, so many opportunities are missed. We respond without analysing what the answer is telling us – we praise effort, evaluate correctness and the lesson moves on.

If the feedback you give is to be meaningful, the learner must understand it. What *exactly* was good about that answer? What would have been a better answer and why would that have been a better answer?

*See meta-analysis of teaching strategies research by Prof. John Hattie and Dr Robert Marzano (helpfully interpreted in **Evidence-Based Teaching** by Geoff Petty.)

Characteristics of effective feedback

What can you do to make feedback effective?

- Be specific rather than general. *'That's not a complete answer' is ineffective* – *'You've said what happened; for a full answer you also need to say why'* shows the student how to improve their answer
- Focus on the answer rather than on the person. *'You think well'* is unhelpful. *'When you analysed the result, you looked at all the variables'* helps the answerer and the rest of the class
- When possible, give feedback immediately. Delayed feedback is less effective
- Be concise. Make too many points and your pupils won't be able to act on them
- Talk about the process as well as the product: *'You chose the correct method to solve the equation and used perseverance.'*

Follow these principles and you will *really* make difference to your pupils' learning.

But...but...

Feedback should be positive, specific and developmental.

	Negative	**Positive**
Non-specific	*'You haven't really thought that through have you?*	*'That was a good answer.'*
Specific	*'You didn't look at both sides of the argument.'*	*'That is a good answer - you took into account both points of view. You need to work on presenting your argument in a more logical order.'*

Compare the following sentence with the positive, specific statement above:

*'That is a good answer – you took into account both points of view **but** you need to work on presenting your argument in a more logical order.'*

Do you think the addition of the word *'but'* makes a difference? *But* can dilute a positive comment to the extent that, for some pupils, it negates the positivity entirely.

Goal, medal and mission

As we have seen, good feedback has an enormous effect on achievement. The more specific, the more impact it has on learning.

The Goal is the learning outcome your students are aiming for. It should be established before the questioning session begins and could be in the format of assessment criteria or specific objectives to be met, eg *'Explain your choice and give clear reasons.'*

The Medal is a comment of acknowledgement establishing where the learner is now in relation to the goal. It can relate to the way a learning activity was done successfully (process) as well as what was achieved (product).

The Mission should consider how the gap between goals and medals can be closed. Missions should be challenging yet achievable and can be about process or product.

Medal and mission feedback accepts the student at the level they currently are, irrespective of their relative position in the class.

Cognitive level of the question

Different types of question demand different types of feedback.

Demands of question	Types of feedback
Memory	Be clear whether correct or incorrect. Lead to a correct answer with memory clues.
Understanding, application	Ask for elaboration and explanation: *'Give me an example'*. Evaluate the correctness of factual elements of the answer.
Evaluation, analysis, synthesis	Give feedback on the thinking: *'How did you arrive at that answer?'* Correct any factual inaccuracies.

A dilemma

We know that one of the best ways to turn a question and answer session into a dialogue is for the teacher to withhold judgement about the answer given – thank the student for the contribution and then seek other views, critiques or corroboration.

> But how does that tie in with what I've just read about the importance of immediate feedback?

Dialogic teaching is different from question and answer sessions, and perhaps we have to sacrifice some of the immediacy of feedback for the sake of depth of thinking. Some of the comments in the exchange will provide feedback in their own way. In addition we must make sure that we give the specific feedback at the end of the discussion.

Talk with your pupils about the process. Unless they understand why you are saying *'thank you'* and not *'well done'* every time they give you an answer, they may think that your ambivalence means that they have given a wrong answer.

Wait Time 2

Wait Time 2 is less well known than Wait Time 1, but equally powerful and as simple to implement. Wait Time 2 refers to **the interval between the pupil's answer and the teacher's response.**

As with Wait Time 1, talk to your class about the process – it can seem very strange at first. The time allowed is the same – three to five seconds minimum. Wait Time 2:

- Shows the students that you are taking their responses seriously
- Gives the student time to elaborate or complete an answer
- Enables you to respond more effectively
- Gives the other students time to compare their answer with the one given

If we are seeking to give truly formative feedback, we cannot jump immediately from the pupil's answer to the teacher's feedback.

Suggestion: You might like to make (or ask your pupils to make) posters representing the Wait Time processes, to support a discussion and act as a visual reminder.

The pupil's voice

Don't patronise your pupils by repeating everything they say so that the rest of the class can hear. Instead, teach them to use a public speaking voice when answering questions.

From early in school life children understand the difference between their playground voice and their classroom voice. If you teach them 'the presenting voice', it will be useful in many situations as well as class discussions.

The point of Wait Time 1 is that pupils have time to consider their answer and how they are going to say it. Don't paraphrase unclear responses – ask them to repeat, or ask a follow up question to enable pupils to clarify for themselves.

The teacher's voice

How students interpret your feedback is key to its effectiveness. Choose your words carefully and use a helpful, positive tone. Whether your feedback has impact or not depends on what the pupil thinks you meant, not what you intended. Check that they understand what you have said.

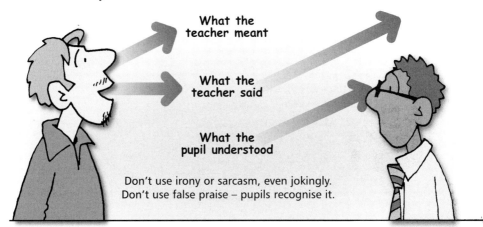

What the
teacher meant

What the
teacher said

What the
pupil understood

Don't use irony or sarcasm, even jokingly.
Don't use false praise – pupils recognise it.

Body language

What you do when a pupil answers a question is as important as what you say. Pupils will read your body language in the same way that they will listen to what you say. And if there is a discrepancy, they will trust what they see over what they hear. You could:

- Look at the pupil who is answering, make eye contact and nod your head
- Lean towards the speaker slightly in encouragement
- When the pupil has finished, maintain eye contact and wait – tilt your head or raise your eyebrows to encourage further response
- Adopt a 'thinking pose' – furrowed brows, a finger in the air or on your chin, pursed lips

When the class is used to 'basketball' dialogue use an open hand gesture to bounce the discussion round the room.

Preparing for the answer

As well as formally planning your questions, think about likely responses and how you will reply. Prepare for expected and deviating answers and think about the most common misunderstandings, errors and misconceptions that pupils of that age are prone to, eg:

If teaching:	Expect some pupils to think that:
Matter	Evaporation and boiling are the same
Decimal fractions	$0.3 + 0.9 = 0.12$ (etc)
Multiplication/division	Commutative law holds for division also, so assuming that because $15 \div 3 = 5$ so $3 \div 15 = 5$
Earth, sun and moon	We experience seasons because of the earth's changing distance to the sun – closer in summer, farther in winter
Pitch	Hitting something harder makes the sound higher

Incorrect answers

When a pupil answers a factual question incorrectly, they are telling you two things – they don't know the answer to your question, and they don't know that their answer belongs to a different question. How do you respond? You could:

- Ask how they came to that answer – the thinking may be praiseworthy and instructional (the intelligent wrong answer)
- Ask how many of the class agree – thumbs up or down (this will let you know whether this is a common misconception or an individual error)
- Ask why they think the answer is right and ask others to evaluate its correctness
- Give the question to which their answer is correct, and ask *your* question again: 'If the question had been *'What city do we live in?'* yes the answer would have been London. But the question was *'What borough do we live in?'* Try again.'
- Collect a range of answers, then ask the class to vote – this allows the student to change their mind
- Ask a follow-up question that leads the student to understand the error – *'but if that's true, then ...'*

Don't be sarcastic or dismissive; express surprise or dismay; attempt empty 'face-saving' as in, *'Nice try, but no.'*

Incomplete answers

Many students will be in the habit of giving brief, minimal answers. They may do this because they have deduced from experience that this is what the teacher wants. Or it may be in the hope that you will be satisfied and move on to someone else.

Encourage your students to justify their response – as far as you're concerned, the reasoning behind the answer is at least as important as the answer itself.

Many teachers move from student to student when questioning, aiming to build up a complete answer. Unfortunately, while the contributors may appear to have built a complete answer between them, no-one has actually done so. Compare the interaction below with the one on the next page:

Teacher:	'Mark, what have we learned so far?'
Mark:	(Gives basic information.)
Teacher:	'That's a good start. Lynn, what can you add?'
Lynn:	(Adds secondary information.)
Teacher:	'Good, we're getting there. Mohammed, what else was there?'
Mohammed:	(Explains the final part of the learning.)

Incomplete answers

Although the previous interaction looks and feels like a complete summary because all the parts fit together and the whole story has been told, none of the students has actually shown that they have complete understanding. Compare it with this:

Teacher: *'Mark, what have we learned so far?'*

Mark: (Gives basic information.)

Teacher: *'That's a good start. And so once we found that out, what did that lead us on to?'*

Mark: (Adds secondary information.)

Teacher: *'Yes, we learned A and then B. And those pieces of information led us on to something else didn't they? Now tell us the whole thing, from the beginning.'*

Mark: (Gives full account.)

Teacher: *'Thank you. Lynn, do you think Mark gave a full account there? Is there anything you would have added or said differently?'*

Socratic questioning techniques can be useful here (see page 117). The quality of discourse is improved, the examination of the matter at hand is deepened and your students are trained to give more complete answers.

Muddled answers and pinpoint questions

A major use for questioning is to diagnose a difficulty. It can be frustrating to witness a pupil floundering and the temptation is to 'help' overcome the difficulty by giving clues. However, it is much better to diagnose the cause of the blockage and help the student to find the solution.

Pinpoint questioning is a highly effective way of uncovering the misunderstanding or missing information and lets you use scaffolding to guide the student to discover the way forward for themselves.

Pupil-speak can be very effective here – other students may be able to provide an explanation that corrects the misunderstanding. Check with the original student that the explanation makes sense to them, then ask a similar question that lets them demonstrate their new understanding.

Focus questioning

Sometimes teachers ask a question that is too big. Perhaps the pupils don't have the expected background knowledge, or don't see the connection between the question and the things they already know. **Focus questions** can lead students through the steps of the thinking. This helps to develop confidence and pupils reveal which stages were causing difficulty.

A year four class was thinking about designs for a wildlife area in the school grounds. In the early stages the teacher asked buzz groups (page 92) to work on the question:

'What design features should be included to attract as much wildlife as possible?'

Despite the teacher clarifying 'design features' the pupils were floundering, unable to see where to begin. The teacher used a series of focus questions to bring known information into working memory and to help the pupils see the connections between the specific and the general.

Focus questions

- *What do you remember from our work on habitat?*
- *What animals did we find on our hunt?*
- *Where did we find them?*
- *What conditions do they seem to like?*
- *What other creatures might we be able to attract?*
- *What conditions do they need? How could we provide them?*
- *Were there any areas where we found no creatures? What conditions did they have?*

The penny dropped for more and more pupils as this line of questioning went on. The teacher was careful to make sure that someone from each group answered one of the questions. Her summary, *'So you know about the kind of place each of the animals likes'* encouraged them to synthesise what they already knew (but didn't realise was relevant) to address the original question.

The ensuing group discussions were rich and productive. The teacher smartly changed the focus of the plenary from habitat information to a discussion about learning to learn techniques and what to do when you are stuck for an answer.

Follow-up questions

Earlier, we looked at basketball questioning and the effectiveness of creating class dialogue. When you have a wide repertoire of follow-up questions at your disposal you can turn even the most mundane answer back on itself and push the thinking forward. This approach will be familiar to those who know the Socratic approach, or Philosophy for Children (P4C). It means moving away from teacher as transmitter to teacher as facilitator, devil's advocate and argument-stirrer.

Transmitter → **Facilitator**

In the interests of equality and inclusion most teachers ask questions of individual pupils in turn. Try asking the pupil who answered a series of follow-up questions before moving to someone else. They may feel like they are being interrogated if they are not used to this way of working so, as with other new strategies, you might want to explain what you're going to try beforehand. For the pupil, the approach can seem confrontational and challenging, so keep the mood light, make it clear that you are testing, not disagreeing. Once in the habit, pupils will think through their responses more deeply and be prepared to deal with speculation and uncertainty.

Follow-up question prompts

Here are some sample follow-up question prompts. Try them with your colleagues as well as your pupils.

Let's clarify your statement	*'What do you mean by..?'* *'Can you give me an example...?'*
Let's dig into your reasoning	*'How do you know?'* *'What are your reasons?'*
Let's look at it another way	*'You said...but what if....?'* *'What's the difference between that and...?'*
Let's think about the implications	*'If that's true, what might be the result?'* *'If that's true, then isn't it also true that...?'*
Let's look again at the question	*'Are we any closer to answering the question?'* *'How does Malia's answer help us?'*

Pitfalls in responding to questions

This chapter has shown the importance and potential of the way you respond to pupils' answers, the importance of feedback, the use of Wait Time 2, your response to misunderstandings and incomplete answers and the importance of follow up questions. Even the best-constructed questions can go to waste if they are not followed up effectively.

Don't
- Allow incorrect answers to go uncorrected
- Miss the implication of an answer
- Miss an opportunity to build an answer into a dialogue
- Interrupt a thoughtful pause in order to 'rescue' a pupil too soon
- Show disappointment at an answer you hoped was going to be more promising
- Paraphrase an answer to correct a mistake
- Give undeserved praise or praise 'ability'
- Give non-specific feedback
- Use irony or sarcasm
- Respond too quickly

Raising Questions

 The Questioning Environment

 Framing Questions

 Delivering the Question

 Responding to the Answer

 Improving Your Practice

Improving Your Practice

Monitoring

The questioning process is often intuitive and in the full flow of a good class discussion can be intense. With questions and answers flowing and split-second decisions being made about what type of question to ask, how to phrase it succinctly, how to pitch it right and who to ask, you may well remember the feeling of a good session, but you are unlikely to remember enough detail to analyse how and why it was successful.

Recording a session and evaluating it can be really useful, particularly when you have a good understanding of the nature of questioning and you are aware of how powerful it can be. If possible, pairing up with a colleague and watching each other is even more effective.

On the following pages are some **quantitative questions,** which will be easy enough to count. Following that is something more **qualitative** which may be trickier to answer, but will really get you thinking.

You

Record a section of a lesson where you have planned a series of questions, or work with a colleague to peer assess your questioning technique.

This set of questions looks at what *you* did.

How many questions did you ask in ten minutes? ☐
How many were open / closed? ☐
For how many questions did you allow more than five seconds Wait Time 1? ☐
For how many questions did you allow more than five seconds Wait Time 2? ☐
Do you accept student responses in a neutral manner or do you use verbal rewards? ☐
How many of the questions were follow-ups to the previous answer? ☐
What was the largest number of 'bounces' you got (pose, pause, pounce, bounce)? ☐
Do you make questions short and clear, using straightforward language? ☐
Were you able to invite a response using body language? ☐
Did you avoid responding to hands up? ☐
Table tennis or basketball? ☐
How many follow-up questions to the same pupil? ☐

Pupils

Here is a quantitative checklist looking at what your pupils did.

How many different children contributed? ☐
Are they the same ones as last lesson? ☐
Did anyone refuse / was anyone unable to answer? ☐
What proportion of answers were one word? ☐
Was anyone ridiculed? ☐
How many pupils justified their answer? (*I think… because…*) ☐
How many answers missed the point of the question? ☐
How many pupils gave partially thought-through answers? ☐
How many pupils made a legitimate challenge to another pupil? ☐
How many times did you hear *I agree / disagree because…*? ☐
Did the pupils speak with clear voices? ☐

Reflection

What effect does knowing that you're assessing yourself have on the questions you ask?

Did your questions move pupils' thinking in terms of the learning objectives? □
Did your questions increase in challenge? □
To what extent do you pre-plan key questions you want to ask during the lesson? □
Did you plan and ask a series of questions? □
What was the outcome? □
What kinds of questions do you ask most? □
Do you accept student responses in a neutral manner or do you use verbal rewards? □
Do you sometimes ask big questions? □
Do you vary the response type, eg TPS, whiteboards, buzz groups? □
To what extent do your questions encourage students to listen to each other's responses? □
To what extent do your questions promote self-evaluation by your students? □

What was the most effective question you asked this week?

Heads of department, subject leaders, SMT

Now that you've looked at your own questioning skills, how about across the school?

You could start by making sure that:

- Your schemes of work contain examples of effective questions
- Your learning and teaching policy incorporates good practice in questioning
- Your professional development sessions include questioning techniques
- Lesson observations specifically evaluate the use of questions
- Teachers have the opportunity to focus on questioning in action research projects

Suggested reading

Classroom Questioning 101: A Pedagogy for Better Questioning
by Gerardo Hannel. Kindle Edition, 2011

Concept-Based Curriculum and Instruction for the Thinking Classroom
by H. Lynn Erickson. Corwin Press, 2007

Evidence-Based Teaching: A Practical Approach (2nd Edition)
by Geoff Petty. Nelson Thornes, 2009

Exemplary Classroom Questioning: Practices to Promote Thinking and Learning
by Marie Menna Pagliaro. Rowman and Littlefield Education, 2011

Questioning in the Secondary School
by E. C. Wragg and G. Brown. Routledge Falmer, 2001

Teaching Thinking: Philosophical Enquiry in the Classroom (2nd Edition)
by Robert Fisher. Continuum, 2003

Thinking Through Quality Questioning: Deepening Student Engagement
by Jackie Acree Walsh and Beth Dankert Sattes. Corwin Press, 2011

http://mindsetonline.com/
Carol Dweck – Mindset

Reading research references for page 73:

The Nature of Literacy Instruction in Ten Grade-4/5 Classrooms in Upstate New York.
Pressley, M. et al (1998). Scientific Studies of Reading, 2, 159-19.

What Classroom Observations Reveal about Reading Comprehension Instruction.
Durkin, D. (1978-9). Reading Research Quarterly, 14, 481-533.

About the author

Gorden Pope

Gorden specialises in provision for able, gifted and talented students, and in the development of thinking skills and creativity. He believes that the key to pupils' success is having enthusiastic, skilled and confident teachers. Gorden began teaching in the late '80s, having studied for his BEd (Hons) as a mature student. After 10 years in a variety of primary schools he moved to Local Authority advisory work in Inner London working with primary and secondary schools.

He then ran his own company providing consultancy to headteachers and leadership teams, and running training sessions in schools, teachers' centres and at conferences. He is currently working at the Institute of Education as a Tutor in Professional Practice. Gorden recently completed his MEd researching the extent to which professional development planning contributes to school improvement.

You can contact Gorden at gordenpope@gmail.com

Order Form

Your details

Name _____

Position _____

School _____

Address _____

_____

_____

Telephone _____

Fax _____

E-mail _____

VAT No. (EC only) _____

Your Order Ref _____

Please send me:

		No. copies
Questioning Technique	Pocketbook	☐
_____	Pocketbook	☐
_____	Pocketbook	☐
_____	Pocketbook	☐

Order by Post

Teachers' Pocketbooks

Laurel House, Station Approach
Alresford, Hants. SO24 9JH UK

Order by Phone, Fax or Internet

Telephone: +44 (0)1962 735573
Facsimile: +44 (0)1962 733637
Email: sales@teacherspocketbooks.co.uk
Web: www.teacherspocketbooks.co.uk

Customers in USA should contact:

2427 Bond Street, University Park, IL 60466
Tel: 866 620 6944   Facsimile: 708 534 7803
Email: mp.orders@ware-pak.com
Web: www.Teacherspocketbooks.com

Pocketbooks – available in both paperback and digital formats

Teachers' Titles:

Accelerated Learning

Anger & Conflict Management

Asperger Syndrome

Assessment & Learning

Behaviour Management

Boys, Girls & Learning

Challenging Behaviours

Coaching & Reflecting

Collaborative Learning

Creative Teaching

Differentiation

Drama for Learning

Dyslexia

Dyspraxia/DCD

EAL

Eating Disorders

Effective Classroom Communication

Emotional Literacy

Form Tutor's

Gifted & Talented

Handwriting

Head of Department's

Inclusion

Jobs & Interviews

Learning & the Brain

Learning to Learn

Lesson Observation

Literacy Across the Curriculum

Managing Workload

Outstanding Lessons

P4C

Primary Headteacher's

Primary Teacher's

Pupil Mentoring

Questioning Technique

Restorative Justice

Secondary Teacher's

Stop Bullying

Teaching Assistant's

Teaching Thinking

Selected Management Titles:

Appraisals

Assertiveness

Coaching

Developing People

Emotional Intelligence

Energy & Well-being

Icebreakers

Impact & Presence

Influencing

Leadership

Managing Change

Meetings

Memory

Mentoring

Motivation

NLP

Openers & Closers

People Manager's

Performance Management

Personal Success

Positive Mental Attitude

Presentations

Problem Behaviour

Resolving Conflict

Succeeding at Interviews

Stress

Storytelling

Tackling Difficult Conversations

Teambuilding Activities

Teamworking

Time Management

Trainer's

Vocal Skills

Workplace Politics